STATEMENT FOR THE RECORD

WORLDWIDE THREAT ASSESSMENT
of the
US INTELLIGENCE COMMUNITY

February 13, 2018

INTRODUCTION

Chairman Burr, Vice Chairman Warner, Members of the Committee, thank you for the invitation to offer the United States Intelligence Community's 2018 assessment of threats to US national security. My statement reflects the collective insights of the Intelligence Community's extraordinary women and men, whom I am privileged and honored to lead. We in the Intelligence Community are committed every day to providing the nuanced, independent, and unvarnished intelligence that policymakers, warfighters, and domestic law enforcement personnel need to protect American lives and America's interests anywhere in the world.

The order of the topics presented in this statement does not necessarily indicate the relative importance or magnitude of the threat in the view of the Intelligence Community.

Information available as of 8 February 2018 was used in the preparation of this assessment.

CONTENTS

FOREWORD

Competition among countries will increase in the coming year as major powers and regional aggressors exploit complex global trends while adjusting to new priorities in US foreign policy. The risk of interstate conflict, including among great powers, is higher than at any time since the end of the Cold War. The most immediate threats of regional interstate conflict in the next year come from North Korea and from Saudi-Iranian use of proxies in their rivalry. At the same time, the threat of state and nonstate use of weapons of mass destruction will continue to grow.

- Adversaries and malign actors will use all instruments of national power—including information and cyber means—to shape societies and markets, international rules and institutions, and international hot spots to their advantage.

- China and Russia will seek spheres of influence and to check US appeal and influence in their regions. Meanwhile, US allies' and partners' uncertainty about the willingness and capability of the United States to maintain its international commitments may drive them to consider reorienting their policies, particularly regarding trade, away from Washington.

- Forces for geopolitical order and stability will continue to fray, as will the rules-based international order. New alignments and informal networks—outside traditional power blocs and national governments—will increasingly strain international cooperation.

Tension within many countries will rise, and the threat from Sunni violent extremist groups will evolve as they recoup after battlefield losses in the Middle East.

- Slow economic growth and technology-induced disruptions in job markets are fueling populism within advanced industrial countries and the very nationalism that contributes to tension among countries.

- Developing countries in Latin America and Sub-Saharan Africa face economic challenges, and many states struggle with reforms to tamp down corruption. Terrorists and criminal groups will continue to exploit weak state capacity in Africa, the Middle East, and Asia.

- Challenges from urbanization and migration will persist, while the effects of air pollution, inadequate water, and climate change on human health and livelihood will become more noticeable. Domestic policy responses to such issues will become more difficult—especially for democracies—as publics become less trusting of authoritative information sources.

GLOBAL THREATS

CYBER THREATS

The potential for surprise in the cyber realm will increase in the next year and beyond as billions more digital devices are connected—with relatively little built-in security—and both nation states and malign actors become more emboldened and better equipped in the use of increasingly widespread cyber toolkits. The risk is growing that some adversaries will conduct cyber attacks—such as data deletion or localized and temporary disruptions of critical infrastructure—against the United States in a crisis short of war.

- In 2016 and 2017, state-sponsored cyber attacks against Ukraine and Saudi Arabia targeted multiple sectors across critical infrastructure, government, and commercial networks.

- Ransomware and malware attacks have spread globally, disrupting global shipping and production lines of US companies. The availability of criminal and commercial malware is creating opportunities for new actors to launch cyber operations.

- We assess that concerns about US retaliation and still developing adversary capabilities will mitigate the probability of attacks aimed at causing major disruptions of US critical infrastructure, but we remain concerned by the increasingly damaging effects of cyber operations and the apparent acceptance by adversaries of collateral damage.

Adversaries and Malign Actors Poised for Aggression

Russia, China, Iran, and North Korea will pose the greatest cyber threats to the United States during the next year. These states are using cyber operations as a low-cost tool of statecraft, and we assess that they will work to use cyber operations to achieve strategic objectives unless they face clear repercussions for their cyber operations. Nonstate actors will continue to use cyber operations for financial crime and to enable propaganda and messaging.

- The use of cyber attacks as a foreign policy tool outside of military conflict has been mostly limited to sporadic lower-level attacks. Russia, Iran, and North Korea, however, are testing more aggressive cyber attacks that pose growing threats to the United States and US partners.

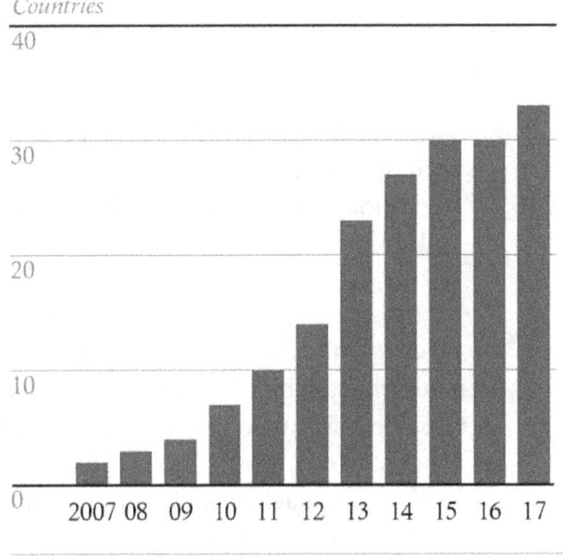

Russia. **We expect that Russia will conduct bolder and more disruptive cyber operations during the next year, most likely using new capabilities against Ukraine.** The Russian Government is likely to build on the wide range of operations it is already conducting, including disruption of Ukrainian energy-distribution networks, hack-and-leak influence operations, distributed denial-of-service attacks, and false flag operations. In the next year, Russian intelligence and security services will continue to probe US and allied critical infrastructures, as well as target the United States, NATO, and allies for insights into US policy.

China. **China will continue to use cyber espionage and bolster cyber attack capabilities to support national security priorities.** The IC and private-sector security experts continue to identify ongoing cyber activity from China, although at volumes significantly lower than before the bilateral US-China cyber commitments of September 2015. Most detected Chinese cyber operations against US private industry are focused on cleared defense contractors or IT and communications firms whose products and services support government and private sector networks worldwide. China since 2015 has been advancing its cyber attack capabilities by integrating its military cyber attack and espionage resources in the Strategic Support Force, which it established in 2015.

Iran. **We assess that Iran will continue working to penetrate US and Allied networks for espionage and to position itself for potential future cyber attacks, although its intelligence services primarily focus on Middle Eastern adversaries—especially Saudi Arabia and Israel.** Tehran probably views cyberattacks as a versatile tool to respond to perceived provocations, despite Iran's recent restraint from conducting cyber attacks on the United States or Western allies. Iran's cyber attacks against Saudi Arabia in late 2016 and early 2017 involved data deletion on dozens of networks across government and the private sector.

North Korea. **We expect the heavily sanctioned North Korea to use cyber operations to raise funds and to gather intelligence or launch attacks on South Korea and the United States.** Pyongyang probably has a number of techniques and tools it can use to achieve a range of offensive effects with little or no warning, including distributed denial of service attacks, data deletion, and deployment of ransomware.

- North Korean actors developed and launched the WannaCry ransomware in May 2017, judging from technical links to previously identified North Korean cyber tools, tradecraft, and operational infrastructure. We also assess that these actors conducted the cyber theft of $81 million from the Bank of Bangladesh in 2016.

Terrorists and Criminals. **Terrorist groups will continue to use the Internet to organize, recruit, spread propaganda, raise funds, collect intelligence, inspire action by followers, and coordinate operations.** Given their current capabilities, cyber operations by terrorist groups mostly likely would result in personally identifiable information (PII) disclosures, website defacements, and denial-of-service attacks against poorly protected networks. Transnational criminals will continue to conduct for-profit cyber-enabled crimes, such as theft and extortion against US networks. We expect the line between criminal and nation-state activity to become increasingly blurred as states view cyber criminal tools as a relatively inexpensive and deniable means to enable their operations.

WEAPONS OF MASS DESTRUCTION AND PROLIFERATION

State efforts to modernize, develop, or acquire weapons of mass destruction (WMD), their delivery systems, or their underlying technologies constitute a major threat to the security of the United States, its deployed troops, and its allies. Both state and nonstate actors have already demonstrated the use of chemical weapons in Iraq and Syria. Biological and chemical materials and technologies—almost always dual-use—move easily in the globalized economy, as do personnel with the scientific expertise to design and use them for legitimate and illegitimate purposes. Information about the latest discoveries in the life sciences also diffuses rapidly around the globe, widening the accessibility of knowledge and tools for beneficial purposes and for potentially nefarious applications.

Russia

Russia has developed a ground-launched cruise missile (GLCM) that the United States has declared is in violation of the Intermediate-Range Nuclear Forces (INF) Treaty. Despite Russia's ongoing development of other Treaty-compliant missiles with intermediate ranges, Moscow probably believes that the new GLCM provides sufficient military advantages to make it worth risking the political repercussions of violating the INF Treaty. In 2013, a senior Russian administration official stated publicly that the world had changed since the INF Treaty was signed in 1987. Other Russian officials have made statements complaining that the Treaty prohibits Russia, but not some of its neighbors, from developing and possessing ground-launched missiles with ranges between 500 and 5,500 kilometers.

China

The Chinese People's Liberation Army (PLA) continues to modernize its nuclear missile force by adding more survivable road-mobile systems and enhancing its silo-based systems. This new generation of missiles is intended to ensure the viability of China's strategic deterrent by providing a second-strike capability. China also has tested a hypersonic glide vehicle. In addition, the PLA Navy continues to develop the JL-2 submarine-launched ballistic missile (SLBM) and might produce additional JIN-class nuclear-powered ballistic missile submarines. The JIN-class submarines—armed with JL-2 SLBMs—give the PLA Navy its first long-range, sea-based nuclear capability. The Chinese have also publicized their intent to form a triad by developing a nuclear-capable next-generation bomber.

Iran and the Joint Comprehensive Plan of Action

Tehran's public statements suggest that it wants to preserve the Joint Comprehensive Plan of Action because it views the JCPOA as a means to remove sanctions while preserving some nuclear capabilities. Iran recognizes that the US Administration has concerns about the deal but expects the other participants—China, the EU, France, Germany, Russia, and the United Kingdom—to honor their commitments. Iran's implementation of the JCPOA has extended the amount of time Iran would need to produce enough fissile material for a nuclear weapon from a few months to about one year, provided Iran continues to adhere to the deal's major provisions. The JCPOA has also enhanced the transparency of Iran's nuclear activities, mainly by fostering improved access to Iranian nuclear facilities for the IAEA and its investigative authorities under the Additional Protocol to its Comprehensive Safeguards Agreement.

Iran's ballistic missile programs give it the potential to hold targets at risk across the region, and Tehran already has the largest inventory of ballistic missiles in the Middle East. Tehran's desire to deter the United States might drive it to field an ICBM. Progress on Iran's space program, such as the launch of the Simorgh SLV in July 2017, could shorten a pathway to an ICBM because space launch vehicles use similar technologies.

North Korea

North Korea will be among the most volatile and confrontational WMD threats to the United States over the next year. North Korea's history of exporting ballistic missile technology to several countries, including Iran and Syria, and its assistance during Syria's construction of a nuclear reactor—destroyed in 2007—illustrate its willingness to proliferate dangerous technologies.

In 2017 North Korea, for the second straight year, conducted a large number of ballistic missile tests, including its first ICBM tests. Pyongyang is committed to developing a long-range, nuclear-armed missile that is capable of posing a direct threat to the United States. It also conducted its sixth and highest yield nuclear test to date.

We assess that North Korea has a longstanding BW capability and biotechnology infrastructure that could support a BW program. We also assess that North Korea has a CW program and probably could employ these agents by modifying conventional munitions or with unconventional, targeted methods.

Pakistan

Pakistan continues to produce nuclear weapons and develop new types of nuclear weapons, including short-range tactical weapons, sea-based cruise missiles, air-launched cruise missiles, and longer-range ballistic missiles. These new types of nuclear weapons will introduce new risks for escalation dynamics and security in the region.

Syria

We assess that the Syrian regime used the nerve agent sarin in an attack against the opposition in Khan Shaykhun on 4 April 2017, in what is probably the largest chemical weapons attack since August 2013. We continue to assess that Syria has not declared all the elements of its chemical weapons program to the Chemical Weapons Convention (CWC) and that it has the capability to conduct further attacks. Despite the creation of a specialized team and years of work by the Organization for the Prohibition of Chemical Weapons (OPCW) to address gaps and inconsistencies in Syria's declaration, numerous issues remain unresolved. The OPCW-UN Joint Investigative Mechanism (JIM) has attributed the 4 April 2017 sarin attack and three chlorine attacks in 2014 and 2015 to the Syrian regime. Even after the attack on Khan Shaykhun, we have continued to observe allegations that the regime has used chemicals against the opposition.

ISIS

We assess that ISIS is also using chemicals as a means of warfare. The OPCW-UN JIM concluded that ISIS used sulfur mustard in two attacks in 2015 and 2016, and we assess that it has used chemical weapons in numerous other attacks in Iraq and Syria.

TERRORISM

Sunni violent extremists—most notably ISIS and al-Qa'ida—pose continuing terrorist threats to US interests and partners worldwide, while US-based homegrown violent extremists (HVEs) will remain the most prevalent Sunni violent extremist threat in the United States. Iran and its strategic partner Lebanese Hizballah also pose a persistent threat to the United States and its partners worldwide.

Sunni Violent Extremism

Sunni violent extremists are still intent on attacking the US homeland and US interests overseas, but their attacks will be most frequent in or near conflict zones or against enemies that are more easily accessible.

- Sunni violent extremist groups are geographically diverse; they are likely to exploit conflict zones in the Middle East, Africa, and Asia, where they can co-mingle terrorism and insurgency.

- ISIS and al-Qa'ida and their respective networks will be persistent threats, as will groups not subordinate to them, such as the Haqqani Taliban Network.

Sunni Violent Extremists' Primary Operating Areas as of 2017

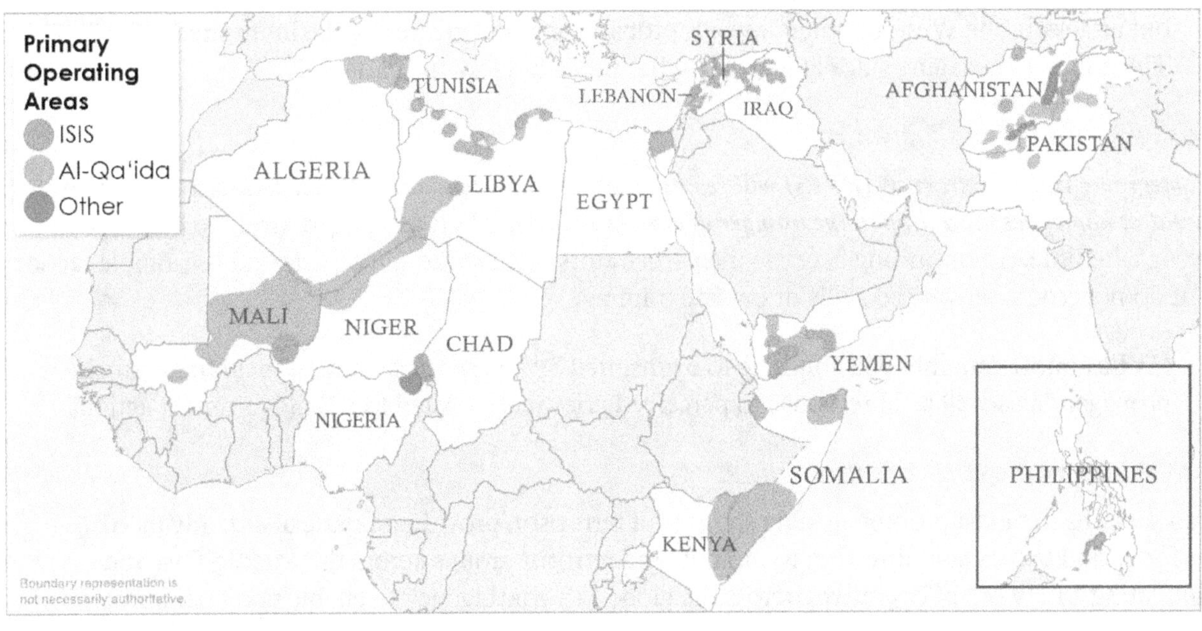

ISIS

Over the next year, we expect that ISIS is likely to focus on regrouping in Iraq and Syria, enhancing its global presence, championing its cause, planning international attacks, and encouraging its members and sympathizers to attack in their home countries. ISIS's claim of having a functioning caliphate that governs populations is all but thwarted.

- ISIS core has started—and probably will maintain—a robust insurgency in Iraq and Syria as part of a long-term strategy to ultimately enable the reemergence of its so-called caliphate. This activity will challenge local CT efforts against the group and threaten US interests in the region.

- ISIS almost certainly will continue to give priority to transnational terrorist attacks. Its leadership probably assesses that, if ISIS-linked attacks continue to dominate public discourse, the group's narrative will be buoyed, it will be difficult for the counter-ISIS coalition to portray the group as defeated, and the coalition's will to fight will ultimately weaken.

- Outside Iraq and Syria, ISIS's goal of fostering interconnectivity and resiliency among its global branches and networks probably will result in local and, in some cases, regional attack plans.

Al-Qa'ida

Al-Qa'ida almost certainly will remain a major actor in global terrorism because of the combined staying power of its five affiliates. The primary threat to US and Western interests from al-Qa'ida's global network through 2018 will be in or near affiliates' operating areas. Not all affiliates will have the intent and capability to pursue or inspire attacks in the US homeland or elsewhere in the West.

- Al-Qa'ida's affiliates probably will continue to dedicate most of their resources to local activity, including participating in ongoing conflicts in Afghanistan, Somalia, Syria, and Yemen, as well as attacking regional actors and populations in other parts of Africa, Asia, and the Middle East.

- Al-Qa'ida leaders and affiliate media platforms almost certainly will call for followers to carry out attacks in the West, but their appeals probably will not create a spike in inspired attacks. The group's messaging since at least 2010 has produced few such attacks.

Homegrown Violent Extremists

Homegrown violent extremists (HVEs) will remain the most prevalent and difficult-to-detect Sunni terrorist threat at home, despite a drop in the number of attacks in 2017. HVE attacks are likely to continue to occur with little or no warning because the perpetrators often strike soft targets and use simple tactics that do not require advanced skills or outside training.

- HVEs almost certainly will continue to be inspired by a variety of sources, including terrorist propaganda as well as in response to perceived grievances related to US Government actions.

Iran and Lebanese Hizballah

Iran remains the most prominent state sponsor of terrorism, providing financial aid, advanced weapons and tactics, and direction to militant and terrorist groups across the Middle East and cultivating a network of operatives across the globe as a contingency to enable potential terrorist attacks.

Lebanese Hizballah has demonstrated its intent to foment regional instability by deploying thousands of fighters to Syria and by providing weapons, tactics, and direction to militant and terrorist groups. Hizballah probably also emphasizes its capability to attack US, Israeli, and Saudi Arabian interests.

COUNTERINTELLIGENCE AND FOREIGN DENIAL AND DECEPTION

The United States will face a complex global foreign intelligence threat environment in 2018. We assess that the leading state intelligence threats to US interests will continue to be Russia and China, based on their services' capabilities, intent, and broad operational scope. Other states in the Near East, South Asia, East Asia, and Latin America will pose local and regional intelligence threats to US interests. For example, Iranian and Cuban intelligence and security services continue to view the United States as a primary threat.

Penetrating the US national decisionmaking apparatus and the Intelligence Community will remain primary objectives for numerous foreign intelligence entities. Additionally, the targeting of national security information and proprietary information from US companies and research institutions involved with defense, energy, finance, dual-use technology, and other areas will remain a persistent threat to US interests.

Nonstate entities, including international terrorists and transnational organized crime groups, are likely to continue to employ and improve their intelligence capabilities, including human, technical, and cyber means. As with state intelligence services, these nonstate entities recruit sources and perform physical and technical surveillance to facilitate their illicit activities and to avoid detection and capture.

Trusted insiders who disclose sensitive or classified US Government information without authorization will remain a significant threat in 2018 and beyond. The sophistication and availability of information technology that increases the scope and impact of unauthorized disclosures exacerbate this threat.

Russia and Influence Campaigns

Influence operations, especially through cyber means, will remain a significant threat to US interests as they are low-cost, relatively low-risk, and deniable ways to retaliate against adversaries, to shape foreign perceptions, and to influence populations. Russia probably will be the most capable and aggressive source of this threat in 2018, although many countries and some nonstate actors are exploring ways to use influence operations, both domestically and abroad.

We assess that the Russian intelligence services will continue their efforts to disseminate false information via Russian state-controlled media and covert online personas about US activities to encourage anti-US political views. Moscow seeks to create wedges that reduce trust and confidence in democratic processes, degrade democratization efforts, weaken US partnerships with European allies, undermine Western sanctions, encourage anti-US political views, and counter efforts to bring Ukraine and other former Soviet states into European institutions.

- Foreign elections are critical inflection points that offer opportunities for Russia to advance its interests both overtly and covertly. The 2018 US mid-term elections are a potential target for Russian influence operations.

- At a minimum, we expect Russia to continue using propaganda, social media, false-flag personas, sympathetic spokespeople, and other means of influence to try to exacerbate social and political fissures in the United States.

EMERGING AND DISRUPTIVE TECHNOLOGY

New technologies and novel applications of existing technologies have the potential to disrupt labor markets and alter health, energy, and transportation systems. We assess that technology developments—in the biotechnology and communications sectors, for example—are likely to outpace regulation, which could create international norms that are contrary to US interests and increase the likelihood of technology surprise. Emerging technology and new applications of existing technology will also allow our adversaries to more readily develop weapon systems that can strike farther, faster, and harder and challenge the United States in all warfare domains, including space.

- The widespread proliferation of artificial intelligence (AI)—the field of computer science encompassing systems that seek to imitate aspects of human cognition by learning and making decisions based on accumulated knowledge—is likely to prompt new national security concerns; existing machine learning technology, for example, could enable high degrees of automation in labor-intensive activities such as satellite imagery analysis and cyber defense. Increasingly capable AI tools, which are often enabled by large amounts of data, are also likely to present socioeconomic challenges, including impacts on employment and privacy.

- New biotechnologies are leading to improvements in agriculture, health care, and manufacturing. However, some applications of biotechnologies may lead to unintentional negative health effects, biological accidents, or deliberate misuse.

- The global shift to advanced information and communications technologies (ICT) will increasingly test US competitiveness because aspiring suppliers around the world will play a larger role in developing new technologies and products. These technologies include next-generation, or 5G, wireless technology; the internet of things; new financial technologies; and enabling AI and big data for predictive analysis. Differences in regulatory and policy approaches to ICT-related issues could impede growth and innovation globally and for US companies.

- Advanced materials could disrupt the economies of some commodities-dependent exporting countries while providing a competitive edge to developed and developing countries that create the capacity to produce and use the new materials. New materials, such as nanomaterials, are often developed faster than their health and environmental effects can be assessed. Advances in manufacturing, particularly the development of 3D printing, almost certainly will become even more accessible to a variety of state and nonstate actors and be used in ways contrary to our interests.

TECHNOLOGY ACQUISITIONS AND STRATEGIC ECONOMIC COMPETITION

Persistent trade imbalances, trade barriers, and a lack of market-friendly policies in some countries probably will continue to challenge US economic security. Some countries almost certainly will continue to acquire US intellectual property and propriety information illicitly to advance their own economic and national security objectives.

- China, for example, has acquired proprietary technology and early-stage ideas through cyber-enabled means. At the same time, some actors use largely legitimate, legal transfers and relationships to gain access to research fields, experts, and key enabling industrial processes that could, over time, erode America's long-term competitive advantages.

SPACE AND COUNTERSPACE

Continued global space industry expansion will further extend space-enabled capabilities and space situational awareness to nation-state, nonstate, and commercial space actors in the coming years, enabled by the increased availability of technology, private-sector investment, and growing international partnerships for shared production and operation. All actors will increasingly have access to space-derived information services, such as imagery, weather, communications, and positioning, navigation, and timing for intelligence, military, scientific, or business purposes. Foreign countries—particularly China and Russia—will continue to expand their space-based reconnaissance, communications, and navigation systems in terms of the numbers of satellites, the breadth of their capability, and the applications for use.

Both Russia and China continue to pursue antisatellite (ASAT) weapons as a means to reduce US and allied military effectiveness. Russia and China aim to have nondestructive and destructive counterspace weapons available for use during a potential future conflict. We assess that, if a future conflict were to occur involving Russia or China, either country would justify attacks against US and allied satellites as necessary to offset any perceived US military advantage derived from military, civil, or commercial space systems. Military reforms in both countries in the past few years indicate an increased focus on establishing operational forces designed to integrate attacks against space systems and services with military operations in other domains.

Russian and Chinese destructive ASAT weapons probably will reach initial operational capability in the next few years. China's PLA has formed military units and begun initial operational training with counterspace capabilities that it has been developing, such as ground-launched ASAT missiles. Russia probably has a similar class of system in development. Both countries are also advancing directed-energy weapons technologies for the purpose of fielding ASAT weapons that could blind or damage sensitive space-based optical sensors, such as those used for remote sensing or missile defense.

Of particular concern, Russia and China continue to launch "experimental" satellites that conduct sophisticated on-orbit activities, at least some of which are intended to advance counterspace capabilities. Some technologies with peaceful applications—such as satellite inspection, refueling, and repair—can also be used against adversary spacecraft.

Russia and China continue to publicly and diplomatically promote international agreements on the nonweaponization of space and "no first placement" of weapons in space. However, many classes of weapons would not be addressed by such proposals, allowing them to continue their pursuit of space warfare capabilities while publicly maintaining that space must be a peaceful domain.

TRANSNATIONAL ORGANIZED CRIME

Transnational organized criminal groups and networks will pose serious and growing threats to the security and health of US citizens, as well as to global human rights, ecological integrity, government revenues, and efforts to deal with adversaries and terrorists. In the most severe cases abroad, criminal enterprises will contribute to increased social violence, erode governments' authorities, undermine the integrity of international financial systems, and harm critical infrastructure.

Drug Trafficking

Transnational organized criminal groups supply the dominant share of illicit drugs consumed in the United States, fueling high mortality rates among US citizens.

- Americans in 2016 died in record numbers from drug overdoses, 21 percent more than in 2015.

- Worldwide production of cocaine, heroin, and methamphetamine is at record levels. US mortality from potent synthetic opioids doubled in 2016, and synthetic opioids have become a key cause of US drug deaths.

- Mexican criminal groups will continue to supply much of the heroin, methamphetamine, cocaine, and marijuana that cross the US-Mexico border, while China-based suppliers ship fentanyls and fentanyl precursors to Mexico-, Canada-, and US-based distributors or sell directly to consumers via the Internet.

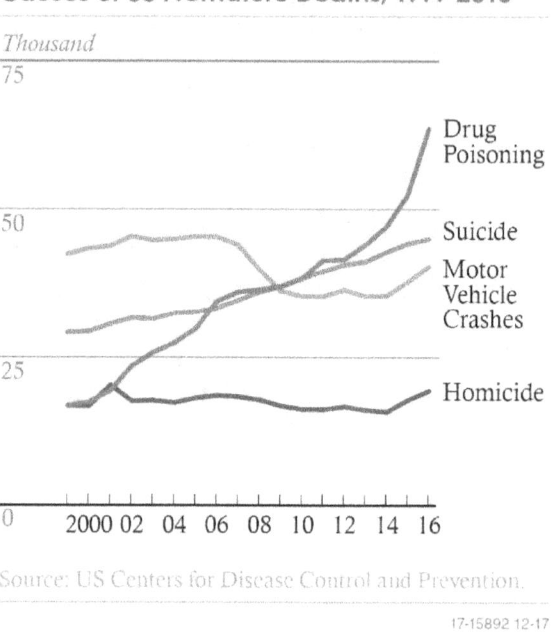

Broader Threats From Transnational Crime

Transnational organized criminal groups, in addition to engaging in violence, will continue to traffic in human beings, deplete natural resources, and siphon money from governments and the global economy.

- Human trafficking will continue in virtually every country. International organizations estimate that about 25 million people are victims.

- The FBI assesses that US losses from cybercrime in 2016 exceeded $1.3 billion, and some industry experts predict such losses could cost the global economy $6 trillion by 2021.

- Criminal wildlife poaching, illegal fishing, illicit mining, and drug-crop production will continue to threaten economies, biodiversity, food supply security, and human health. For example, academic studies show that illicit mining alone adds some 650 to 1,000 tons of toxic mercury to the ecosystem each year.

- Transnational organized criminal groups probably will generate more revenue from illicit activity in the coming year, which the UN last estimated at $1.6-$2.2 trillion for 2014.

Global growth in 2018—projected by the IMF to rise to 3.9 percent—is likely to become more broadly based, but growth remains weak in many countries, and inflation is below target in most advanced economies. The relatively favorable outlook for real economic growth suggests little near-term risk of unfavorable deficit-debt dynamics among the advanced economies. Supportive financial conditions and improving business sentiment will help to drive economic activity in advanced countries. China's growth may decelerate as the property sector cools and if Beijing accelerates economic reforms. India's economy is expected to rebound after headwinds from taxation changes and demonetization, and the continuing upswing in emerging and developing economies could be tempered by capital outflows from a stronger dollar and monetary policy normalization in the United States and Europe.

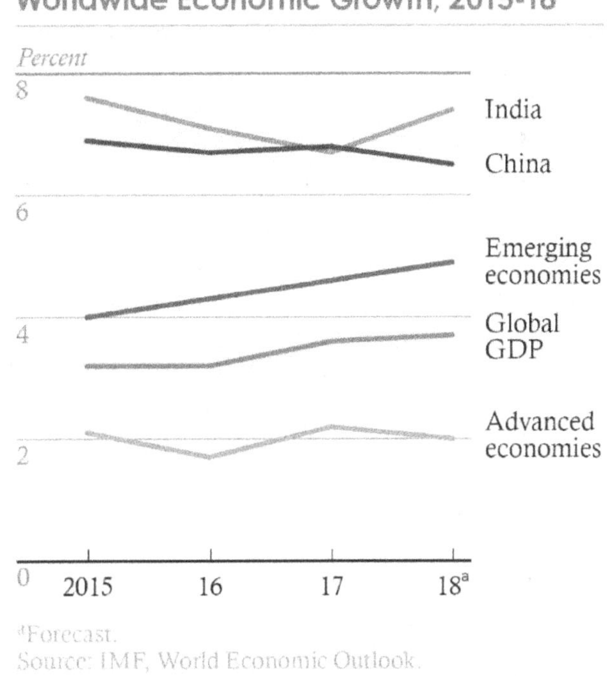

Oil-exporting countries continue to suffer from the late-2014 oil price drop, and their economic woes are likely to continue, with broader negative implications. Subdued economic growth, combined with sharp increases in North American oil and gas production, probably will continue putting downward pressure on global energy prices, harming oil-exporting economies. The US Energy Information Administration forecasts that 2018 West Texas Intermediate and Brent prices will average $58 and $62 per barrel, respectively, far below the average annual prices of $98 and $109 in 2013.

- Low oil prices and production declines—along with poor economic policies—have pushed Venezuela and the state-owned oil company, Petroleos de Venezuela, to miss debt payments, putting them in selective default.

- Saudi Arabia and other Persian Gulf oil exporters have experienced sharp increases in budget deficits, forcing governments to issue debt and enact politically unpopular fiscal reforms, such as cuts to subsidies, social programs, and government jobs.

- In Africa, declining oil revenue, mismanagement, and inadequate policy responses to oil price shocks have contributed to Angolan and Nigerian fiscal problems, currency strains, and deteriorating foreign exchange reserves.

- OPEC member countries and select non-OPEC producers, including Russia, in early 2017 committed to cut oil production in order to lift prices, with compliance likely to be offset somewhat as Libya or Nigeria—both are exempt from the deal—are able to resume production.

HUMAN SECURITY

Governance shortfalls, violent conflict, environmental stresses, and increased potential for a global health crisis will create significant risks to human security, including high levels of human displacement and migration flows.

Governance and Political Turbulence

Domestic and foreign challenges to democracy and institutional capacity will test governance quality globally in 2018, especially as competitors manipulate social media to shape opinion. Freedom House reported the 11th consecutive year of decline in "global freedom" in 2017, and nearly one-quarter of the countries registering declines were in Europe.

- While the number of democracies has remained steady for the past decade, some scholars suggest the quality of democracy has declined.

- We note that more governments are using propaganda and misinformation in social media to influence foreign and domestic audiences.

- The number and sophistication of government efforts to shape domestic views of politics have increased dramatically in the past 10 years. In 2016, Freedom House identified 30 countries, including the Philippines, Turkey, and Venezuela, whose governments used social media to spread government views, to drive agendas, and to counter criticism of the government online.

Poor governance, weak national political institutions, economic inequality, and the rise of violent nonstate actors all undermine states' abilities to project authority and elevate the risk of violent—even regime-threatening—instability and mass atrocities.

Environment and Climate Change

The impacts of the long-term trends toward a warming climate, more air pollution, biodiversity loss, and water scarcity are likely to fuel economic and social discontent—and possibly upheaval—through 2018.

- The past 115 years have been the warmest period in the history of modern civilization, and the past few years have been the warmest years on record. Extreme weather events in a warmer world have the potential for greater impacts and can compound with other drivers to raise the risk of humanitarian disasters, conflict, water and food shortages, population migration, labor shortfalls, price shocks, and power outages. Research has not identified indicators of tipping points in climate-linked earth systems, suggesting a possibility of abrupt climate change.

- Worsening air pollution from forest burning, agricultural waste incineration, urbanization, and rapid industrialization—with increasing public awareness—might drive protests against authorities, such as those recently in China, India, and Iran.

- Accelerating biodiversity and species loss—driven by pollution, warming, unsustainable fishing, and acidifying oceans—will jeopardize vital ecosystems that support critical human systems. Recent estimates suggest that the current extinction rate is 100 to 1,000 times the natural extinction rate.

- Water scarcity, compounded by gaps in cooperative management agreements for nearly half of the world's international river basins, and new unilateral dam development are likely to heighten tension between countries.

Human Displacement

Global displacement almost certainly will remain near record highs during the next year, raising the risk of disease outbreaks, recruitment by armed groups, political upheaval, and reduced economic productivity. Conflicts will keep many of the world's refugees and internally displaced persons from returning home.

Health

The increase in frequency and diversity of reported disease outbreaks—such as dengue and Zika—probably will continue through 2018, including the potential for a severe global health emergency that could lead to major economic and societal disruptions, strain governmental and international resources, and increase calls on the United States for support. A novel strain of a virulent microbe that is easily transmissible between humans continues to be a major threat, with pathogens such as H5N1 and H7N9 influenza and Middle East Respiratory Syndrome Coronavirus having pandemic potential if they were to acquire efficient human-to-human transmissibility.

- The frequency and diversity of disease outbreaks have increased at a steady rate since 1980, probably fueled by population growth, travel and trade patterns, and rapid urbanization. Ongoing global epidemics of HIV/AIDS, malaria, and tuberculosis continue to kill millions of people annually.

- Increasing antimicrobial resistance, the ability of pathogens—including viruses, fungi, and bacteria—to resist drug treatment, is likely to outpace the development of new antimicrobial drugs, leading to infections that are no longer treatable.

- The areas affected by vector-borne diseases, including dengue, are likely to expand, especially as changes in climatological patterns increase the reach of the mosquito.

- The World Bank has estimated that a severe global influenza pandemic could cost the equivalent of 4.8 percent of global GDP—more than $3 trillion—and cause more than 100 million deaths.

REGIONAL THREATS

EAST ASIA

China

China will continue to pursue an active foreign policy—especially in the Asia Pacific region—highlighted by a firm stance on its sovereignty claims in the East China Sea (ECS) and South China Sea (SCS), its relations with Taiwan, and its pursuit of economic engagement across the region. Regional tension will persist due to North Korea's nuclear and missile programs and simmering tension over territorial and maritime disputes in the ECS and SCS. China will also pursue efforts aimed at fulfilling its ambitious Belt and Road Initiative to expand China's economic reach and political influence across Eurasia, Africa, and the Pacific through infrastructure projects.

North Korea

North Korea's weapons of mass destruction program, public threats, defiance of the international community, confrontational military posturing, cyber activities, and potential for internal instability pose a complex and increasing threat to US national security and interests.

In the wake of accelerated missile testing since 2016, North Korea is likely to press ahead with more tests in 2018, and its Foreign Minister said that Kim may be considering conducting an atmospheric nuclear test over the Pacific Ocean. Pyongyang's commitment to possessing nuclear weapons and fielding capable long-range missiles, all while repeatedly stating that nuclear weapons are the basis for its survival, suggests that the regime does not intend to negotiate them away.

Ongoing, modest improvements to North Korea's conventional capabilities continue to pose a serious and growing threat to South Korea and Japan. Despite the North Korean military's many internal challenges and shortcomings, Kim Jong Un continues to expand the regime's conventional strike options with more realistic training, artillery upgrades, and close-range ballistic missiles that improve North Korea's ability to strike regional US and allied targets with little warning.

Southeast Asia

Democracy and human rights in many Southeast Asian countries will remain fragile in 2018 as autocratic tendencies deepen in some regimes and rampant corruption and cronyism undermine democratic values. Countries in the region will struggle to preserve foreign policy autonomy in the face of Chinese economic and diplomatic coercion.

- Cambodian leader Hun Sen will repress democratic institutions and civil society, manipulate government and judicial institutions, and use patronage and political violence to guarantee his rule beyond the 2018 national election. Having alienated Western partners, Hun Sen will rely on Beijing's political and financial support, drawing Cambodia closer to China as a result.

- The crisis resulting from the exodus of more than 600,000 Rohingyas from Burma to Bangladesh will threaten Burma's fledgling democracy, increase the risk of violent extremism, and provide openings for Beijing to expand its influence.

- ***In the Philippines, President Duterte will continue to wage his signature campaign against drugs, corruption, and crime.*** Duterte has suggested he could suspend the Constitution, declare a "revolutionary government," and impose nationwide martial law. His declaration of martial law in Mindanao, responding to the ISIS-inspired siege of Marawi City, has been extended through the end of 2018.

- ***Thailand's leaders have pledged to hold elections in late 2018, but the new Constitution will institutionalize the military's influence.***

MIDDLE EAST AND NORTH AFRICA

Iran

Iran will seek to expand its influence in Iraq, Syria, and Yemen, where it sees conflicts generally trending in Tehran's favor, and it will exploit the fight against ISIS to solidify partnerships and translate its battlefield gains into political, security, and economic agreements.

- Iran's support for the Popular Mobilization Committee (PMC) and Shia militants remains the primary threat to US personnel in Iraq. We assess that this threat will increase as the threat from ISIS recedes, especially given calls from some Iranian-backed groups for the United States to withdraw and growing tension between Iran and the United States.

- In Syria, Iran is working to consolidate its influence while trying to prevent US forces from gaining a foothold. Iranian-backed forces are seizing routes and border crossings to secure the Iraq-Syria border and deploying proregime elements and Iraqi allies to the area. Iran's retaliatory missile strikes on ISIS targets in Syria following ISIS attacks in Tehran in June were probably intended in part to send a message to the United States and its allies about Iran's improving military capabilities. Iran is pursuing permanent military bases in Syria and probably wants to maintain a network of Shia foreign fighters in Syria to counter future threats to Iran. Iran also seeks economic deals with Damascus, including deals on telecommunications, mining, and electric power repairs.

- In Yemen, Iran's support to the Huthis further escalates the conflict and poses a serious threat to US partners and interests in the region. Iran continues to provide support that enables Huthi attacks against shipping near the Bab al Mandeb Strait and land-based targets deep inside Saudi Arabia and the UAE, such as the 4 November and 19 December ballistic missile attacks on Riyadh and an attempted 3 December cruise missile attack on an unfinished nuclear reactor in Abu Dhabi.

Iran will develop military capabilities that threaten US forces and US allies in the region, and its unsafe and unprofessional interactions will pose a risk to US Navy operations in the Persian Gulf.

Iran continues to develop and improve a range of new military capabilities to target US and allied military assets in the region, including armed UAVs, ballistic missiles, advanced naval mines, unmanned explosive boats, submarines and advanced torpedoes, and antishipand land-attack cruise missiles. Iran has the largest ballistic missile force in the Middle East and can strike targets up to 2,000 kilometers from Iran's borders. Russia's delivery of the SA-20c SAM system in 2016 has provided Iran with its most advanced long-range air defense system.

- Islamic Revolutionary Guard Corps (IRGC) Navy forces operating aggressively in the Persian Gulf and Strait of Hormuz pose a risk to the US Navy. Most IRGC interactions with US ships are professional, but as of mid-October, the Navy had recorded 14 instances of what it describes as "unsafe and/or unprofessional" interactions with Iranian forces during 2017, the most recent interaction occurring last August, when an unarmed Iranian drone flew close to the aircraft carrier USS Nimitz as fighter jets landed at night. The Navy recorded 36 such incidents in 2016 and 22 in 2015. Most involved the IRGC Navy. We assess that these interactions, although less frequent, will continue and that they are probably intended to project an image of strength and, possibly, to gauge US responses.

Iranian centrist and hardline politicians increasingly will clash as they attempt to implement competing visions for Iran's future. This contest will be a key driver in determining whether Iran changes its behavior in ways favorable to US interests.

- Centrists led by President Hasan Ruhani will continue to advocate greater social progress, privatization, and more global integration, while hardliners will view this agenda as a threat to their political and economic interests and to Iran's revolutionary and Islamic character.

- Supreme Leader Ali Khamenei's views are closer to those of the hardliners, but he has supported some of Ruhani's efforts to engage Western countries and to promote economic growth. The Iranian economy's prospects—still driven heavily by petroleum revenue—will depend on reforms to attract investment, strengthen privatization, and grow nonoil industries, which Ruhani will continue pursuing, much to the dismay of hardliners. National protests over economic grievances in Iran earlier this year have drawn more attention to the need for major reforms, but Ruhani and his critics are likely to use the protests to advance their political agendas.

- Khamenei has experienced health problems in the past few years, and, in an effort to preserve his legacy, he probably opposes moving Iran toward greater political and economic openness. As their relationship has deteriorated since the presidential election last June, Ruhani has tried to mend relations with Khamenei as well as his allies, but, in doing so, he risks failing to make progress on reforms in the near-term.

Syria

The conflict has decisively shifted in the Syrian regime's favor, enabling Russia and Iran to further entrench themselves inside the country. Syria is likely to experience episodic conflict through 2018, even as Damascus recaptures most of the urban terrain and the overall level of violence decreases.

- ***The Syrian opposition's seven-year insurgency is probably no longer capable of overthrowing President Bashar al-Asad or overcoming a growing military disadvantage.*** Rebels probably retain the resources to sustain the conflict for at least the next year.

- ISIS is likely on a downward trajectory in Syria; yet, despite territorial losses, it probably possesses sufficient resources, and a clandestine network in Syria, to sustain insurgency operations through 2018.

- Moscow probably cannot force President Asad to agree to a political settlement that he believes significantly weakens him, unless Moscow is willing to remove Asad by force. While Asad may engage in peace talks, he is unlikely to negotiate himself from power or offer meaningful concessions to the opposition.

- Russia and Iran are planning for a long-term presence, securing military basing rights and contracts for reconstruction and oil and gas exploitation. Iran is also seeking to establish a land corridor from Iran through Syria to Lebanon. The Kurdish People's Protection Unit—the Syrian militia of the Kurdistan Workers' Party (PKK)—probably will seek some form of autonomy but will face resistance from Russia, Iran, and Turkey.

- As of October 2017, there were more than 5 million Syrian refugees in neighboring countries, and an estimated 6.3 million internally displaced. Reconstruction could cost at least $100 billion and take at least 10 years to complete. Asad's battered economy will likely continue to require significant subsidies from Iran and Russia to meet basic expenses.

Iraq

Iraq is likely to face a lengthy period of political turmoil and conflict as it struggles to rebuild, reconstitute the Iraqi state, maintain pressure on ISIS, and rein in the Iranian-backed Shia militias that pose an enduring threat to US personnel.

- The Iraqi Government, which has accrued $120 billion in debt, requires substantial external assistance to cover hundreds of millions of dollars in humanitarian-aid shortfalls and a World Bank estimated $88.2 billion to restore heavily damaged infrastructure, industry, and service sectors in areas retaken from ISIS.

- Prime Minister Haydar al-Abadi's forceful reassertion of Baghdad's authority after the Kurdistan Regional Government's (KRG) independence referendum in September illustrates the divisions among Iraqi leaders over the future of the state. The move to curb Kurdish autonomy was popular among many Arab Shia and Sunnis and may prompt Iraqi leaders to be uncompromising in political reconciliation discussions in order to consolidate votes in the run-up to elections planned for next spring.

- ISIS will remain a terrorist and insurgent threat, and the group will seek to exploit Sunni discontent to conduct attacks and try to regain Iraqi territory. Baghdad will struggle to reorient the Iraqi Security Forces (ISF) from conventional warfare to counterinsurgency and counterterrorism against ISIS while consolidating state control of territory and integrating the Iranian-backed and Shia-dominated Popular Mobilization Committee (PMC).

- There is an increasing risk that some Shia militants will seek to attack US targets in Iraq because they believe that the US security presence is no longer needed, want to reassert Iraqi sovereignty, and support Iran's goal of reducing US influence in Iraq.

Baghdad will have to contend with longstanding and war-hardened ethnosectarian divisions between Shia, Sunnis, and Kurds that were kept in check by the threat from ISIS. Despite ISIS's loss of territory, the social and political challenges that gave rise to the group remain and threaten the cohesion of the Iraqi state.

Yemen

The war in Yemen is likely to continue for the foreseeable future because the Iranian-backed Huthis and the Saudi-led coalition remain far apart on terms for ending the conflict. The death of former Yemeni President Ali Abdallah Salih is only likely to further complicate the conflict as the Huthis and others scramble to win over those who previously backed Salih. We assess that the Huthis will continue to pursue their goals militarily and that, as a result, US allies and interests on the Arabian Peninsula will remain at risk of Huthi missile attacks until the conflict is resolved.

- Continued fighting almost certainly will worsen the vast humanitarian crisis, which has left more than 70 percent of the population—or about 20 million people—in need of assistance and aggravated a cholera outbreak that has reached nearly 1 million confirmed cases. Relief operations are hindered by security and bureaucratic constraints established by both the Huthi-Salih alliance and the Saudi-led coalition and by international funding shortages.

SOUTH ASIA

Afghanistan

The overall situation in Afghanistan probably will deteriorate modestly this year in the face of persistent political instability, sustained attacks by the Taliban-led insurgency, unsteady Afghan National Security Forces (ANSF) performance, and chronic financial shortfalls. The National Unity Government probably will struggle to hold long-delayed parliamentary elections, currently scheduled for July 2018, and to prepare for a presidential election in 2019. The ANSF probably will maintain control of most major population centers with coalition force support, but the intensity and geographic scope of Taliban activities will put those centers under continued strain. Afghanistan's economic growth will stagnate at around 2.5 percent per year, and Kabul will remain reliant on international donors for the great majority of its funding well beyond 2018.

South Asian Threats Challenge
US Security Interests in 2018

- Deteriorating Political/Security Situation
- Militant Support
- India-Pakistan Tensions
- India-China Tensions
- Rohingya Refugee Crisis

Pakistan

Pakistan will continue to threaten US interests by deploying new nuclear weapons capabilities, maintaining its ties to militants, restricting counterterrorism cooperation, and drawing closer to China. Militant groups supported by Islamabad will continue to take advantage of their safe haven in Pakistan to plan and conduct attacks in India and Afghanistan, including against US interests. Pakistan's perception of its eroding position relative to India, reinforced by endemic economic weakness and domestic security issues, almost certainly will exacerbate long-held fears of isolation and drive Islamabad's pursuit of actions that run counter to US goals for the region.

India-Pakistan Tension

Relations between India and Pakistan are likely to remain tense, with continued violence on the Line of Control and the risk of escalation if there is another high-profile terrorist attack in India or an uptick in violence on the Line of Control.

India-China Tension

We expect relations between India and China to remain tense and possibly to deteriorate further, despite the negotiated settlement to their three-month border standoff in August, elevating the risk of unintentional escalation.

Bangladesh-Burma Rohingya Crisis

The turmoil resulting from more than 600,000 Rohingyas fleeing from Burma to Bangladesh increases regional tension and may expand opportunities for terrorist recruitment in South and Southeast Asia. Further operations by Burmese security forces against Rohingya insurgents or sustained violence by ethnic Rakhine militias probably would make it difficult to repatriate Burmese from Bangladesh.

RUSSIA AND EURASIA

Russia

In his probable next term in office, President Vladimir Putin will rely on assertive and opportunistic foreign policies to shape outcomes beyond Russia's borders. He will also resort to more authoritarian tactics to maintain control amid challenges to his rule.

Moscow will seek cooperation with the United States in areas that advance its interests. Simultaneously, Moscow will employ a variety of aggressive tactics to bolster its standing as a great power, secure a "sphere of influence" in the post-Soviet space, weaken the United States, and undermine Euro-Atlantic unity. The highly personalized nature of the Russian political system will enable Putin to act decisively to defend Russian interests or to pursue opportunities he views as enhancing Russian prestige and power abroad.

Russia will compete with the United States most aggressively in Europe and Eurasia, while applying less intense pressure in "outer areas" and cultivating partnerships with US rivals and adversaries—as well as with traditional US partners—to constrain US power and accelerate a shift toward a "multipolar" world. Moscow will use a range of relatively low-cost tools to advance its foreign policy objectives, including influence campaigns, economic coercion, cyber operations, multilateral forums, and measured military force. Russia's slow

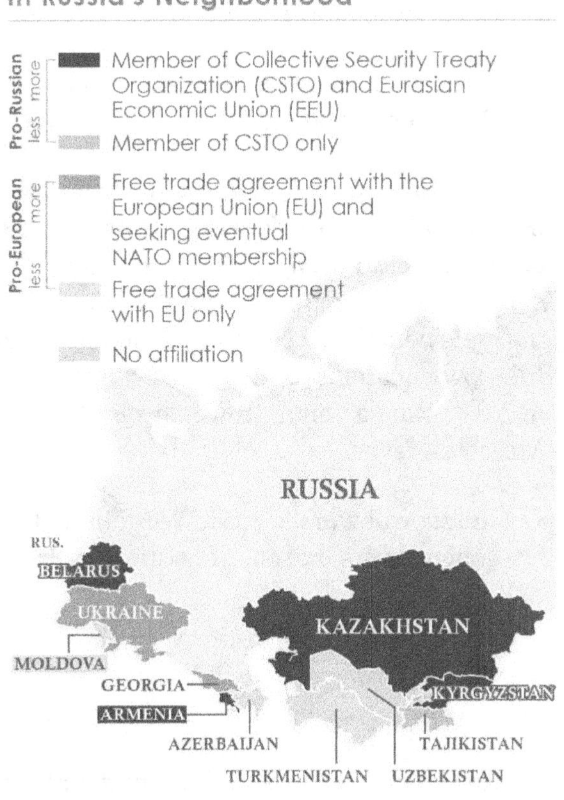

economic growth is unlikely to constrain Russian foreign policy or by itself trigger concessions from Moscow in Ukraine, Syria, or elsewhere in the next year.

President Putin is likely to increase his use of repression and intimidation to contend with domestic discontent over corruption, poor social services, and a sluggish economy with structural deficiencies. He will continue to manipulate the media, distribute perks to maintain elite support, and elevate younger officials to convey an image of renewal. He is also likely to expand the government's legal basis for repression and to enhance his capacity to intimidate and monitor political threats, perhaps using the threat of "extremism" or the 2018 World Cup to justify his actions.

In 2018, Russia will continue to modernize, develop, and field a wide range of advanced nuclear, conventional, and asymmetric capabilities to balance its perception of a strategic military inferiority vis-a-vis the United States.

Ukraine

Ukraine remains at risk of domestic turmoil, which Russia could exploit to undermine Kyiv's pro-West orientation. These factors will threaten Ukraine's nascent economic recovery and potentially lead to changes in its foreign policy that further inflame tension between Russia and the West.

- Popular frustrations with the pace of reforms, depressed standards of living, perceptions of worsening corruption, and political polarization ahead of scheduled presidential and legislative elections in 2019 could prompt early elections.

- Opposition leaders will seek to capitalize on popular discontent to weaken President Petro Poroshenko and the ruling coalition ahead of elections in 2019.

The conflict in eastern Ukraine is likely to remain stalemated and marked by fluctuating levels of violence. A major offensive by either side is unlikely in 2018, although each side's calculus could change if it sees the other as seriously challenging the status quo. Russia will continue its military, political, and economic destabilization campaign against Ukraine to stymie and, where possible, reverse Kyiv's efforts to integrate with the EU and strengthen ties to NATO. Kyiv will strongly resist concessions to Moscow but almost certainly will not regain control of Russian-controlled areas of eastern Ukraine in 2018. Russia will modulate levels of violence to pressure Kyiv and shape negotiations in Moscow's favor.

- Russia will work to erode Western unity on sanctions and support for Kyiv, but the Kremlin is coping with sanctions at existing levels.

Belarus, the Caucasus, Central Asia, Moldova

The Kremlin will seek to maintain and, where possible, expand its influence throughout the former Soviet countries that it asserts are in its self-described sphere of influence.

Russia views Belarus as a critical buffer between itself and NATO and will seek to spoil any potential warming between Minsk and the West. Belarus President Aleksandr Lukashenko will continue close security cooperation with Moscow but will continue to aim for normalized relations with the West as a check on Russia's influence.

Russia's continued occupation of 20 percent of Georgia's territory and efforts to undermine its Western integration will remain the primary sources of Tbilisi's insecurity. The ruling Georgian Dream party is likely to seek to stymie the opposition and reduce institutional constraints on its power.

Tension over the disputed region of Nagorno-Karabakh could devolve into a large-scale military conflict between Armenia and Azerbaijan, which could draw in Russia to support its regional ally. Both sides' reluctance to compromise, mounting domestic pressures, Azerbaijan's steady military modernization, and Armenia's acquisition of new Russian equipment sustain the risk of large-scale hostilities in 2018.

Russia will pressure Central Asia's leaders to reduce engagement with Washington and support Russian-led economic and security initiatives, while concerns about ISIS in Afghanistan will push Moscow to strengthen its security posture in the region. Poor governance and weak economies raise the risk of radicalization—especially among the many Central Asians who travel to Russia or other countries for work—presenting a threat to Central Asia, Russia, and Western societies. China will probably continue to expand outreach to Central Asia—while deferring to Russia on security and political matters—because of concern that regional instability could undermine China's economic interests and create a permissive environment for extremists, which, in Beijing's view, could enable Uighur militant attacks in China.

Moldova's ostensibly pro-European ruling coalition—unless it is defeated in elections planned for November—probably will seek to curb Russian influence and maintain a veneer of European reform while avoiding changes that would damage the coalition's grip on power. The current Moldovan Government probably will move forward on implementing Moldova's EU Association Agreement against the will of openly pro-Russian and Russian-backed President Igor Dodon. Settlement talks over the breakaway region of Transnistria will continue, but progress likely will be limited to small issues.

EUROPE

The European Union and European national governments will struggle to develop common approaches to counter a variety of security challenges, including instability on their periphery, irregular migration to their region, heightened terrorist threats, and Russian influence campaigns, undercutting Western cohesion.

- These concerns are spurring many countries to increase defense spending and enhance capabilities.

- European governments will need to strengthen their counterterrorism regimes to deal with a diverse threat, including ISIS aspirants and returning foreign fighters.

Turkey's counterterrorism cooperation with the United States against ISIS is likely to continue, but thwarting Kurdish regional ambitions will be a foreign policy priority. President Recep Tayyip Erdogan is likely to employ polarizing rhetoric, straining bilateral relations and cooperation on shared regional goals.

Nigeria—the continent's largest economy—will face a security threat from Boko Haram and ISIS West Africa (ISIS-WA) while battling internal challenges from criminal, militant, and secessionist groups. ISIS-WA and Boko Haram are regional menaces, conducting cross-border attacks in Nigeria, Cameroon, Chad, and Niger and posing a threat to Western interests. Meanwhile, militant and secessionist groups in in the southern and central areas of Nigeria are capitalizing on longstanding social and economic grievances as the country nears the 2019 presidential election.

Politically fragile governments in Africa's Sahel region will remain vulnerable to terror attacks in 2018, despite efforts to coordinate their counterterror operations. ISIS and al-Qa'ida–allied groups, along with other violent extremists, will attempt to target Western and local government interests in the region, and a stalled peace process is likely to undercut the presidential election in Mali.

The Ethiopian and Kenyan Governments are likely to face opposition from publics agitating for redress of political grievances. Somalia's recently elected government probably will struggle to project its authority and implement security reforms amid the drawdown of African Union forces in 2018, while al-Shabaab—the most potent terrorist threat to US interests in East Africa—probably will increase attacks.

Clashes between the South Sudanese Government and armed opposition groups will continue, raising the risk of additional mass atrocities as both sides use ethnic militias and hate speech and the government continues its crackdown on ethnic minorities. The South Sudanese are the world's fastest growing refugee population, and the significant humanitarian challenges stemming from the conflict, including severe food insecurity, will strain the resources of neighboring countries hosting refugees.

Sudan is likely to continue some aspects of its constructive engagement with the United States following the suspension of sanctions because it has given priority to shedding its international pariah status and reviving its economy. Khartoum probably will acquiesce to some US requests, such as increasing counterterrorism cooperation and improving humanitarian access, but will be reluctant to take any steps that it perceives jeopardize its national security interests.

Political unrest and security threats across the region are likely to intensify as the Presidents of Burundi and the Democratic Republic of the Congo (DRC) face public and armed opposition to their rule and the Central African Republic (CAR) struggles to cope with a nationwide surge in conflict. Over-stretched UN missions in CAR and DRC are unlikely to stem the rising challenges from their concurrent humanitarian and security crises.

A key feature of the 2018 political environment in Latin America almost certainly will be popular frustration with low economic growth, corruption scandals, and the specter of endemic criminal activity in some countries. Larger and increasingly sophisticated middle classes—with greater access to social media—are demanding more accountability from their governments. Presidential elections, including those in Mexico and Colombia, will occur at a time when support for political parties and governing institutions is at record lows and could bolster the appeal of outsider candidates.

Mexico

Mexicans are focused on presidential and legislative elections scheduled for July 2018, in which corruption, high violence, and a tepid economy will be key issues. The Mexican Government has made slow progress implementing rule-of-law reforms and will continue to rely on the military to lead counternarcotics efforts. Mexico's $1.1 trillion economy benefits from strong economic fundamentals, but uncertainty over trade relationships and higher-than-expected inflation could further slow economic growth. President Enrique Pena Nieto is focusing on domestic priorities, including recovery from the September 2017 earthquakes and managing impacts from potential US policy shifts ahead of the elections. In recent years, Mexican US-bound migration has been net negative but might increase if economic opportunity at home declined.

Central America

Insecurity and lack of economic opportunities likely will remain the principal drivers of irregular migration from the Northern Triangle countries of El Salvador, Guatemala, and Honduras. Homicide rates in these countries remain high, and gang-related violence is still prompting Central Americans to flee.

Venezuela

Economic woes and international diplomatic pressure probably will put political pressure on the Venezuelan Government in 2018. Living standards have declined and shortages of basic goods are driving the increase in Venezuelans seeking asylum in the United States and the region. Venezuela's negotiations with creditors probably will lead to messy legal battles. Venezuela almost certainly will seek to minimize further disruptions to oil production and exports to maintain its critical oil export earnings. Oil prices have increased slightly this year, but crude oil production continues to decline.

Colombia

President Juan Manuel Santos will seek to cement implementation of the Revolutionary Armed Forces of Colombia (FARC) peace accord, as campaigning intensifies for the May 2018 presidential election. The FARC's new political-party status and the uncertainty around the transitional justice reforms will be a factor in the political environment ahead of elections. Substantial budget constraints will slow major programs or policy changes. The influx of FARC dissidents, drug traffickers, and other illegal actors into remote areas will challenge security forces during the next 12 months. Cocaine production in Colombia is at an all-time high, and crop substitution and eradication programs are facing stiff local resistance.

Cuba

Havana will seek to manage President Raul Castro's planned retirement in April 2018. Castro's successor will inherit a stagnant economy and a stalled economic reform process.

Haiti

As President Jovenel Moise begins his second year in office, he will confront competing interests within his government, a vocal opposition, and a fragile economy. Crime and protest activity will test the Haitian National Police following the departure of the UN Stabilization Mission in October 2017 and the transition to a police-only UN mission.